Leaves

by Emily Robertson

PEARSON

Glenview, Illinois • Boston, Massachusetts • Chandler, Arizona
Upper Saddle River, New Jersey

leaf

A leaf from a
willow tree

Leaves give us shade on a sunny day. Leaves are
food for animals and bugs. Leaves are fun to play in.
But why do trees have leaves?

Trees need leaves to make food. Leaves have chlorophyll (KLOR uh fil). Chlorophyll collects sunlight. Water and carbon dioxide (dy AHK syd) change sunlight into sugary water. This water feeds the tree. The way leaves make food is called photosynthesis.

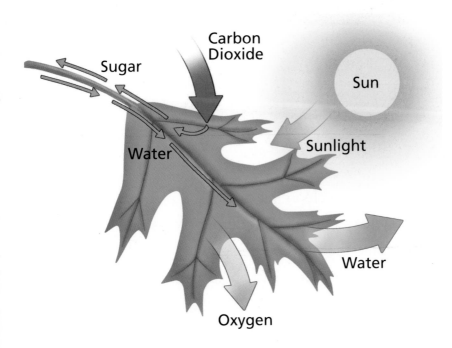

Photosynthesis

ginkgo leaf

Leaves also clean the air.

They take carbon dioxide out of the air. They put oxygen into the air. Oxygen is what people breathe. Leaves help trees. They help people too.

In the fall, the air gets colder. There is less sunlight. Photosynthesis stops. Then the leaves change color. Finally, the leaves die. They fall to the ground.

After that, winter comes. The dead leaves become a part of the soil. They make the soil healthy. This helps plants grow in the spring.

Extend Language **Greek Word Origins**

The word *photosynthesis* means "putting together with light." The prefix *photo-* means "light." Why is this a good name for the way leaves make food?

sweet gum leaf

Read this poem about leaves:

A leaf is a wonder
All year round,
Up in a tree
Or down on the ground.

Green or yellow,
Orange or brown,
A leaf is a wonder
All year round.

In the spring, the sunlight gets stronger. Spring rains come. Trees grow new leaves. Photosynthesis begins again. Trees wake up from their winter sleep.

Glossary

car•bon di•ox•ide
  (KAR bin dy AHK syd),
  **special gas that plants
  use to make food**

chlo•ro•phyll
  (KLOR uh fil), **material
  in leaves that collects
  sunlight and helps
  leaves make food**

ox•y•gen
  (AHK sih jin), **gas that
  animals and people
  breathe in**

pho•to•syn•the•sis
  (foh toh SIN thih sis), **way
  plants use sunlight,
  water, and carbon
  dioxide to make food**